# *MEMORY LANE*

I0461478

## REMINISCE WITH ME THROUGH HEALING POETRY

To schedule a poetry, writing and healing workshop scan QR code or visit www.thegoodlookinbooks.com

Disclaimer:
These are my memories, from my perspective,
and I have tried to represent events as
faithfully as possible.
.

Softcover ISBN:979-8-9865663-1-3
Hardcover ISBN:979-8-9865663-2-0

References: TNoncology.com and
The American Cancer Society

The GoodLook In Books Corp.
www.thegoodlookinbooks.com

# DEDICATION

This book is dedicated to YOU, the beautiful souls who have seen me through this lane of mine. I will start with my mom Magda Rivera-Seabrook and although there were times in my earlier life I didn't understand you, I am thankful for you and your constant support. I am proud of you and I love you. To my biological father Manuel "Happy" Ruiz at this moment I am unaware of where you are but I hope that my energy tells you how much I love you and pray for your safety daily. I always thought our bond will never break but life is so unexpected but I am not angry at you, nor do I blame you, I LOVE YOU. To my Dad Clive Seabrook who adopted me and his soul is in some dog right now lol I can feel it, I Thank you dearly for stepping up and putting up with me. To my oldest brother Carlos who was in the Navy for years, never do I feel as if you were not there for me, I understand you had to save your life and I am forever grateful to have you as my big bro. To my sister Suzan Henriquez it seems as if we always go through our ups and downs but no matter what please understand that I love you and I am thankful for teaching me how to tip a waitress as a child (NO ONE EVER TAUGHT ME THAT) and it means a great deal, thank you for holding my son down when I needed you and much more. To my other brother Edwin Henriquez, we been through so much as kids and I hope that your journey will help you in your growth and help others too, love you. To my brother Clive Seabrook III aka Nuke, man you came into my life when it felt so empty and even though you are older than me I literally took you in as a younger brother and I love you for life, our bond is definitely unbreakable. Last of my siblings but never least Michael Revilla aka Twin, all I am going to say is that I made a promise years ago that NOONE will ever keep me from being in your life ever again and I hope that I have shown you how much you and the kids mean to me. To all my nieces and nephews I hope you know that I value our relationship and I love you, cousins I will start with Lynnette Rivera Cunningham because you have been there for me and our relationship is so important, so close and I am thankful to have you in our lives, sometimes we wonder why other people who should have been aren't but I couldn't see my life without you, Jazzy or Scott. To all my cousins on the Rivera side, Jason, Mikey, Stephen you all have played an important part of my life and I thank you. To my Ruiz side, Jessica, Tanya, David, his wife Barbara, Elizabeth, Titi Evelyn, Aunt Helen, Danny, Lowana and my Uncle David in spirit, my childhood memories with you are the absolute best and I thank you til this day for loving me. Seabrook side my cousin Pop gets super amounts of love, you always support me, always check on me and always tell me how proud you are, well I am proud of you and your Uncle Clive is as well. To my cousins who came from my sons father side of the family, you all have made a special place in my heart for eternity and there are too many to name and too many memories to discuss here but to say a few Sharon, Coco, Paula, Monica, Mikey, Amari, Tre, Dee, Nelly, Quohn, Chris and the rest of you, thank you.
Stewart McCain, thank you for showing me how to level up and see a world that I knew existed but didn't actually know how to see it completely. They say when a student is ready, a teacher will appear and I thank you for the many lessons in this thing called life #LoveAndLight.

CONT'D

To the Alverio family, words can not express how much I appreciate you all being there for me as a child, life was pretty harsh but with you in it, life was easier. To my sis Makia Carter, you know I love you to the moon and back and I pray everyday for your happiness, thank you for always being there, showing up and showing out. Denise Sanchez I pray all your dreams come true and I am thankful for all that we have seen together, laughed about together, cried about and got through together. The Marion Ave family, it is that blocked that help made me who I am today, thank you to those who always held me down and up!

Friends who are more like my family, Della for always checking on me and making sure I keep sending out these messages via poetry and encouraging me, Shariea Perry aka MC Heavyn and the whole Perry family, I love you and thank you for remaining consistent and always being there for me. Jocelyn David-Burch the wife of my cousin Christopher Burch thank you for making sure I did this damn book lol and always giving me ideas and words of encouragement, you are appreciated.

I can go on and on about people who support me so please forgive me if I missed your name, Jo Walker, Sheyla Muniz, Judith Morales, Wil Santiago and their children whom I love as my own, Rasheeda Ali, Nicole Hazard Newton (who edited my book), Michael Jacobs (one of my biggest supporters), Tasha Monique, David Hopper, Tom Ray, Chenia Ayala, Gloria Cunningham, Melanie Archer, Cicely Greaves, Diane Mitchell, Rel Williams (who gave me my 1st show in NYC),Kevin Meggett, Derrick Bonner, Monique Burkhalter and many more.

To my Cali family I met in Georgia that helped me raise my son Veronica aka Vee Boogie, Miguel aka Brother Migwel LOL and the kids I thank you for being my village.

Deidre, Crystal, Mecca Jones and my entire Jones family, I love you and you are my sisters, blood has no say so in this, it's about all that we have been through with each other and how we been there for each other. My Carrasquillo family, I thank you for always being there for me.

My Ghetto Chronicles family Dwhit, Stephen aka Distruck, Brett, JCisco and MC Heavyn again. That show made us family if we were not already and even though some of us may not speak everyday, it is an amazing memory in my life that I would always cherish.

Linda Bonnano aka Litty of Got Checked Records, it is hard to describe what I feel for you in words but thank you for loving and believing in me, you are one of a kind my friend lol.

To my Guns Down Life Up family, James Dobbins, Maria Lopez, John King, the kids involved I have to say that your work, your passion and commitment does not go unnoticed and I thank you for always including me and loving me

Last but not least is my Bronx Regional Family. I won't list all my friends because it is so many but from high school days, to shows, to hurtful events in between YOU all have been there for me. My click "The Sugar Hill Gang" which I already mentioned Deidre and Denise but can't leave out my sister Tranya Kelly AKA Taz AKA the dopest female basketball player around.

To the staff like Wade Williams and Alfred "Smitty" Smith (R.I.P) and to all of my peers that I remain friends with this day, my eyes tear up as I acknowledge you because you have been a major part in my life and I thank you so so much. It brings me great pleasure that even til this day I can count on many of you #Classof1994 and more, I thank you again and I love you.

# INTRODUCTION

Memory Lane was created as a branch off my album which was put together in about one week. I had surely taken some time with creating this baby. I always wanted to create my poetry book, but it had to have more meaning than just being able to read my stories. I wanted to figure out a way to help others get the healing I received when I started writing. I always say, "poetry was my therapy". Although I am the writer for this book, I want you to go down Memory Lane with me and write your feelings down too. Following every poem is a page for you to express your thoughts and/or experiences. For example, you may read one of my poems and it may not have been something you personally went through, but maybe a loved one did, and it still affected you. I want you to write about that and you can choose to put it in poet form or not either way just LET IT OUT. We tend to hold things so much, that it causes us to stay stagnant. It causes us to be angry with others because the choices that they made had an influence on who you became as an adult, how you treat others and most importantly how you treated yourself. Writing and expressing these thoughts onto paper gives it a new meaning and a relief to just be able to let it all out. After writing you need to read it and accept it, figure out how you can forgive and move on. Is it easy? Nothing great comes easy but I can assure you, it is ALL worth it. Imagine making a difference in your life or the lives of others?

I really want to make this short and sweet and have you ride through this journey with me. In hopes that when you are done with this book, we can get together (no matter where you're at), sit down and express these feelings verbally and hey maybe even poetically (it doesn't all have to rhyme) it just has to mean something to you, it has to be expressed even if it hurts but you will learn that there is always love at the end of it, you know that self-love and nothing is better than that.

Yall Ready? Let's Go!

# TABLE OF CONTENTS

# WHY ALL THESE MIXED UP FEELINGS?

I remember when things were so confusing not knowing why all these things happened in my life. Then the blame game began starting with childhood, the parents and then thinking that this may be all my fault. I looked at everything I been through and asked myself why am I feeling all these mixed up feelings?

# ~MIXED UP FEELINGS~

I'm content but uncomfortable I'm happy but I'm sad
At times I feel all alone this makes me so mad
Can someone tell me what are all these feelings about
I know that I'm loved and I am not without
There's just something that's bothering me inside my heart
This began from way back when don't know how to start
Maybe it started from seeing my mom being abused
Or me as a teenage rebel with nothing to lose
Could it have been my brother was gone for all those years
It be nights after nights sad and crying those tears
Or was it living in a shelter young, cold and hungry
Promising myself when I grow up that this won't be me
Could it have been the times that I was touched in certain places
By people in your family and everyday you have to see their faces
Or is it that my father stopped seeing me for his new wife
I'm your only child, I'd never thought I wouldn't be in your life
Or was it leaving my mom's home at the age of seventeen
Found myself in a situation with a boy who turned out to be mean
So was it the broken noses and the black eyes that were on my face
Me fighting back but was so confused and in a terrible headspace
Or was it when my mom finally found love with the man who became my Dad
And he passed away and is missed is another reason Im sad
Well I guess there may be may be a lot of reasons
Why I am having all of these unknown mixed up feelings
What I do know is that through all these dealings
That I learned to face my demons and started on my healing
So I needed to let out all of these emotions
So my mind could be clear from what was once a commotion

## What have you been feeling these past few years?
### Let it out!

# WHERE WAS YOUR PEACE AND COMFORT AS A TEEN?

Have you ever felt comfortable being anywhere else besides your home?

Yea I had a space like that it was called Bronx Regional High School. I graduated in 1994 and that was the school I even met my son's father at. Sometimes we may not have our parents there but we always have to know someone is there to help, we just have to be open to receive it.

So I want to start off this memory with a dedication to Smitty (R.I.P) and all the teachers at my high school. I would not have gotten through so many things in my life if it were not for you all.

# ~SMITTY~

Coming into Bronx Regional I know I speak for many others
We came in with our guards up, confused and unsure of who we were as sisters
and brothers
We came in with trust issues, anger and pain that we didn't understand
We were kicked out of our schools, had problems at home but this is where our
new life began
Smitty had a class called conflict resolution
Where we discussed our problems but more importantly came up with solutions
This was the first time I felt as if we had a voice
Normally it's sit down, be quiet, you do what I say! We weren't given a choice
Smitty made sure we were not a product of Project X
Something that was designed to see us fail, stay a mess to keep us from
becoming a success
He seen something bigger in us, in our spirits, seen and felt our pain
He made sure we knew our worth, supported us, I don't recall him to ever
complain
This was the man that I felt comfortable in telling him all my "secrets"
Kept things to myself for so many years so no one could take advantage of my
weakness
But with Smitty it was just comfort in knowing he wasn't going to judge us
He made it clear that there was actually somebody in our lives that genuinely
loved us
To his children I want to apologize if you were left without a snack or lunch
money from time to time
Because boy oh boy we stood in his pockets from the dollars to the dimes
Between him and his right hand man Sam I don't know how they managed
To take care of us, take care of home and be all of our parents
Bronx Regional was our safe haven it's where we felt protected
Because of Smitty and many other teachers we never felt neglected
I'm sorry that he is gone in the physical but I can assure you his soul is content
He completed his mission and took on the world and was indeed "God sent"

Did you seek comfort at home or
outside of home as a teen? Write about your experiences.

# BRINGING LIFE INTO THIS WORLD

I met my son's father at my high school.
I was 22 years old when I had my son and I did not realize how young I was until my son turned 22 and it HIT me! Wow, I was my son's age when I had him? I had no clue on what it was to parent but I did know that I wanted to be different with him. I wanted to give him the life and opportunities that I didn't have, but it was a process in me getting to that point of removing those generational curses. I am thankful for my son's understanding and love.

# ~MY SON!~

April 28th, 1999
That's the day that my life turned around
10lbs 9ounces its my baby boy
Named him Dazje my new bundle of joy
They brought him to me I just held him and cried
Did not want him to have a childhood like mine
His Dad was around for about 2 years after his birth
It's hard learning to put someone else besides yourself first
Unfortunate for my son but I had to leave his Dad
I know he wanted us together but our relationship was bad
Hopefully as my son gets older he will understand
just because his Dad is not around he will still be a good man.
To do what is right and not follow others
To appreciate what I have done for him as his mother
Take responsibility for the choices he makes
Learn to deal with others and point out the real from the fake
Do not depend or rely on anyone else
To always live Godly and to love himself first
To believe in his power and be nothing but the best
Want him to value himself as more not anything less
Because life can be hard and not always fair
One thing he can count on is that I will always be there
Through the ups and downs, Through the thick and the thin
And of course when he has his first girlfriend
It surely isn't easy raising a boy to a man
But for sure I'm gonna do everything that I can
So before I go I must let him know
that he is my mind, my heart and my soul.

What are your thoughts about bringing life into this world?

# MY APOLOGIES FOR NOT KNOWING

So yea I had my son and that poem was written when he wasn't even a teenager and he is now 23 years of age. I am reflecting looking at that poem and saying wow I'm impressed with how he really is all of the things I wished, hoped and worked on with him. However I put my son through a lot and one was going into another unhealthy relationship shortly after my separation with his father. I am so sorry for everything that I've done, I didn't do and didn't know how to do. I am sorry for putting you in situations that made you make the wrong decisions in life. I thank you for not judging me, holding anything against me, supporting me, loving me and believing in me.

# ~THANKFUL FOR THE PAIN~

Wow I thought I found someone to love me

For a minute there I really was happy

He cared for my son as if he were his

Not only that he showed his love for his kids

Took that into consideration damn he's a good man

Made it seem like he would put the world in my hands

We became closer on a deeper level

Thought he was spiritual but not knowing he's the devil

Things started to change I was confused

What happened to the love I was getting abused

Verbally, physically and mentally too

This wasn't right I didn't know what to do

Packed my clothes got up and out

Had to leave him fast without a doubt

Moved to Virginia hoping that I'll make it

Then here he calls with the crying and fake biz

Thought he was sincere and needed a better life

Told him come down I got you I'm your wife

I couldn't see him hurting and didn't want to make

things worst

Not thinking of myself or my son who should've came first

So we get back together and of course its sweet

Making plans so we can get back on our feet

I'm working 2 jobs trying to make things right

Getting home tired late at night

Sometimes I get home and my son's homework ain't done

It's 10 @night what was he doing when he should've

been helping my son

CONT'D

11

That was a small thing there's a whole lot more

Come to find out he was screwing some whore

Which happened to be my neighbors sister

She looked greasy and nasty how could he even kiss her

Not only that I was pregnant with his baby

Messed up shit I thought I was his lady

He stole my money to spend on this chick

2 days with no food ain't this some shit

He left his BMW in front of the crib

Bad move bad move so you know what I did

Put syrup in his tank and cut up all the tires

Scratched up his hood and cut up all the wires

Threw all of his clothes and shoes in the trash

That's what he got for messing with my ass

Got my son packed up the car

Didn't have no money couldn't go too far

Went to a friends she gave me some cash

Just enough for a room and some gas

Drove to North Carolina not knowing where to go

Asking God to guide me because I surely did not know

Confused and crying how could he do this to me

I have my son and I'm pregnant this really couldn't be

I feel like I'm about to go crazy and I'm really going to lose it

How in the world can I get through this

Driving back to NY I'm contemplating this

Whether I should keep this baby or terminate it

By the time I reached up I made my decision

Asking God to forgive me and for the permission

CONT'D

So I stopped by my cousins she was surprised

She knew something was wrong we just hugged and we cried

Told her what happened and what I needed to do

She said Kim do what you feel is right for you

I went to the clinic and got it done

A 2 day procedure was not at all fun

Now my son comes back into play

He was expecting to be a big brother what was I to say

My son was hurt, not with me but at this jerk

For not even trying to make things work

Yes the road was rough but I got back on my feet

Got me a job in about three weeks

Then around two months I got my own crib

The one who helped me was the mother of his two kids

Now my son and her kids consider themselves to be brothers

Thank god we are not the typical baby mothers

We look out for each other and the kids as well

We understand and respect one another cause he also put
her through hell

So I am thankful for the pain, the hurt, the tears and the stress

Because without it I could not appreciate my happiness

What was one of the most painful experiences you faced
and how did you overcome it or trying to.

# WHO WAS YOUR FRIEND THROUGH THE PAIN?

During that time of the relationship man it was crazy. He was a big time drug dealer and we hustled and partied. He never did anything other than weed until one day....

Now I used to party but not to the extent of when we both started getting high together, I was very much on point with my habits meaning I could have an eight ball for weeks and not touch it unless I wanted to and there were times I even gave shit away.

But back to that one day....

We were having an argument and he stated, "I'm going to sniff all this shit!" my response was, "PLEASE DO NOT BECAUSE EVERYONE CAN'T HANDLE IT."

Then it was too late and it became toxic from there....

because Her Name is Cocaine

# ~HER NAME IS COCAINE~

Those sexy lines she's white and I can feel her in my veins

No its not Heroine but her name is Cocaine

I took that first hit and that's how it all starts

Wow I feel that racing and that speeding of my heart

I want more of her so I am not going to stop

So yeah for this one I'm going to spend I need to go cop

At this point in my life there was nothing to lose

I felt neglected but she was the one I would not refuse

She knew how to get in my mind straight to my brain

I'm loving this chick her name is Cocaine

She is my friend I can't sleep so she keeps me awake

She is the only one who heals my heart that happens to ache

So she stands by my side near my bed to be exact

I turn over to look at her damn she is stacked

I get closer cause I really do want to feel her inside me

I know she wants me too she wants to be inside my body

I'm loving how she feels its driving me insane

Cause she's that chick and her name is Cocaine

I haven't felt this in a while she gives me a rush

I like what she does she's making me blush

I'm smoking and drinking with her all through the night

I'm thinking she's got my back and with her I'll always be alright

But I'm in this zone that I'm realizing I don't wanna be

She has turned me to this other person I am no longer me

She stopped me from eating food I can't even stand the smell

I thought she was my heaven but she really was my hell

CONT'D

.

Didn't even realize all the weight that I had lost
Not knowing half of the things that this relationship cost
Almost lost my friends, my family and even my home
But if I stop messing with Cocaine I'm gonna feel alone
What do I do? How do I leave her behind?
I want her near me cause she is never hard to find
She follows me to the club, the streets and even my job
I want to feel her cause she is the one to make my heart throb
How do I get out of this relationship it's so conflicting
That chick Cocaine she's so Got Damn addicting
I had to come to my senses and decided to let her go
I wanted nothing to do with her or her alias Ms. Blow
I found out she was talking crap behind my back
She was scheming with my ex and that dude called Crack
It only took that to see that we had to come to an end
She was trying to mess me over she was never my friend
So Ms. Cocaine aka Ms. Blow I no longer need you around
I thought you was keeping me up but no longer can you keep me down

.

## Ever experienced substance abuse or know someone who has?
## How did that effect you?

## IMAGINE
## WHAT IT IS TO
## BE LOVED?

You ever just imagine meeting someone who is just perfect and not perfect in things but just perfect for you?

After leaving a bad relationship it's hard to trust. How does one move on and forgive not just yourself but the person or persons who have done things to you to make you how you are now. Confused, scared, nervous, intimidated or even worse, bitter and angry. Sometimes its nice to just sit back and imagine what he would be like...

## ~I WANT TO KNOW~

I am looking but only from the corner of my eyes

I'm acting as if I don't see acting as if I don't realize

Yes I'm being stubborn in my own little ways

Because being easy is something I don't want to portray

It is the physical attraction that has caught my attention

So what's in his head is he just looking to release his erection

I think he just wants to feel my flesh but I'm ready to build

I'm interested in finding out I want to know what he feels

So maybe now I throw a little smile and give some eye contact

But I'm wondering what does he have and what does he lack

I have these questions that are running through my mind

Lately a good, hardworking, single man has been hard to find

Wondering if he is married or still screwing his baby's mama

I know that I am too old for any type of drama

Is he the type of man who would not dare to commit

I think he has been hurt before in his past relationship

I can see him, I'm not sure who he is but I'm interested in knowing

Is he stuck in this world or does he have the potential of growing

Damn this man is fine and I am so liking his style

I'm second guessing myself. Is it really worth my while?


CONT'D

.

Cause he might be the type to understand when I'm having a bad day
But he also might be the type to give up and just walk away
I am thinking all these thoughts and I don't even know his name
I'm judging because of my past and now I feel ashamed
Maybe he is a good man this is not like it's impossible
He could be the type who takes care of his and is responsible
Maybe he was the type who got caught up in the system
But he has learned from his mistakes and is no longer a victim
I want to know who he is but I am still fighting this feeling
Cause knowing rather than judging is so much more appealing
So I decided I am going to find out start by asking his name
If I don't I might be losing out and now who's the one to blame
He might have questions about myself and who I am
We all have some issues this is something I have to understand
I know that we are all not perfect so what is it that I'm doing
These negative thoughts in my head it's only me that I'm ruining
So we are talking and I'm liking what I'm getting from our conversation
In building anything in this world it has to start with a foundation
I have to put my guard down I have to tear down these walls
Have to learn to move on and no longer will I stall.

.

Have you ever been scared to love? If so why?
If not, what would you tell someone who is?

## THEN IT BECOMES A REALITY. HE DOES EXIST

You are in this mood like the sun is shining everywhere you go.
You meet
someone and they seem to be everything you want and you just
want to be
everything that no one was to you. That feeling of being able to
make someone feel like they never have to worry about being
alone or hurt because you will be right there because you just
Wanna Be!!

# ~I WANNA BE~

I wanna be the voice for when you cannot speak
I wanna be the strength for those days you are weak
I wanna be the light for when all you see is darkness
I wanna be the one to wake you from your unconsciousness
I wanna be your Tylenol for when all you feel is pain
I wanna be your sunshine after all you see is rain
I wanna be your heartbeat when you can't feel your pulse
I wanna be the truth when all you know is false
I wanna be your rhythm for when all you feel are blues
I wanna be your therapy when you start to feel confused
I wanna be your blanket to warm you from the cold
I wanna be your arms when you can no longer hold
I wanna be your feet so that I can walk in your shoes
I wanna be your motion when you are unable to move
I wanna be your future if you are stuck in the past
I wanna show you how to live like every day is your last
I wanna be your garden so I can help you grow
I wanna be your yes when you are used to hearing no
I wanna be your rose petal cause all you feel are thorns
I wanna be your stitch when you happen to feel torn
I wanna be your vitamin when you need your daily dose
I wanna be your vision to show you that you matter most
I wanna be your wings to help you fly high
I wanna be the star that you wish upon in the sky
I wanna be your oxygen so that I can help you breathe
I wanna be the key to your lock to set your spirit free
I wanna be your navigation if you are unsure of which way to go
I wanna be your high if you happen to feel low
I wanna be your music to make you dance inside
I wanna be your journey when you are ready for that ride

What do you wanna be? Whether its for someone else or yourself.

## SO NOW WHAT? WE MEET SOMEONE NEW AND WHAT DO WE DO?

What a good question. How do we move on?

What should we do?

What shouldn't we do?

If we are putting all this work into wanting to be all these things for

someone else but what about yourself?

What about compromising???

even if it's just a little...

I do want to thank Eartha Kitt for the inspiration on this poem

YouTube her video "Compromise"

## ~COMPROMISE~

So when did it become ok to compromise

To accept standards that are lower than what is desired to you

To accept deceit and lies because he looks into your eyes

Thinking that this is the norm or even tolerable

Got you infatuated with his size, the way he works in between your thighs

Now he got you mesmerized got you all dicknotized

So when did it become ok to compromise

As if lust is the same feeling of love not realizing it's a disguise

It's characterized to make your stomach filled with butterflies

Until the reality hits and just for being yourself

You are expected to apologize

Change your whole demeanor, your style and even your smile

When he won't walk and inch for you but you steady traveling miles

All the time, effort and improvises goes unrecognized

Doing things that would have been considered to demoralize

YOU so they criticize and they patronize

Belittling you instead of knowing how to empathize

That you were taught that it was ok to compromise

It's ok to put your feelings to the side

It's ok if you feel denied, It's ok if he doesn't provide

But this is what has been televised. This is nothing but a false advertise

No way should these traits even be glorified

At what point do you take responsibility for loving the woman inside

When do you choose to revive the [if you meant for the word revive to pause, consider putting it on the next line for a natural pause instead of a comma.] soul of a woman who has died?

Heal yourself put the bandages on where they need to be applied

Reorganize, prioritize and stop staying on the backside

Otherwise you will be living your life in compromise

Should one compromise or not? Describe why you feel the way you do.

```
┌─────────────────────────────────┐
│                                 │
│   WE  ALWAYS  SEE               │
│   WHAT  IT  LOOKS               │
│   LIKE  ON  THE                 │
│   OUTSIDE                       │
│                                 │
└─────────────────────────────────┘
```

We like to think that we know what we want by the way we
were taught. Finish school, go to college, get married and
have kids. That is how its designed for **SOME** of us right?
Coming from certain situations it doesn't always work out that
way. We are never taught to find love within self, we are
never taught to look inside and work on that before anything.
Sometimes your vision is not just what you see but also what
you feel.  What is your Vision?

# ~VISION~

I feel like I can't see like I lost my Vision

Not knowing what to do I lost my position

I feel like I was driving and got into a collision

I feel like I can't see like I lost my Vision

I'm confused, scared I can't make a simple decision

I feel like I'm watching my life like it's on television

I feel like I can't see like I lost my Vision

I thought I had a purpose, thought I had a mission'

Why is it that I can't hear, why can't I listen

I feel like I can't see like I lost my Vision

I'm at that point all I know is depression

It's easier to give up its become an addiction

I feel like I can't see like I lost my Vision

The pain is cutting me I have a huge incision

Sick of peoples shit sick of their egotism

I feel like I can't see like I lost my Vision

I feel like being spiritual I don't want a religion

Why is that a problem why is there confliction

I feel like I can't see like I lost my Vision

I feel like I'm tied down with only restriction

At one point I was motivated one point I was driven

I feel like I can't see like I lost my Vision

I don't wanna be seen I just wanna be hidden

I'm not happy was that something I forgot to mention

I feel like I can't see like I lost my Vision

Why my hard work and talents have to be given

I'm ready to shine like after the sun has risen

I feel like I can't see like I lost my Vision

I'm ready for the world, ready for my mission

Ready to take over and claim my position

To heal from all this pain that was once an infliction

Now I have the remedy, now I have the prescription

I feel like I can do anything I don't need your permission

Now I can see clearly now, Thank God for my Vision

What do you see for yourself now and in the future?

## YOU EVER WANTED TO APOLOGIZE TO SOMEONE?

My father passed away from Cancer on December 25,2008.
I have a poem on my arm that I wrote for him but here's another
one with me apologizing to him for being so selfish when I was
younger. When your biological Dad decides to never see you
again and some stranger walks into your life within that next year
it seems like just another person who will do the same. At first I
wasn't very nice but I was just protecting myself the way I knew
how.

# ~SORRY FOR BEING SO SELFISH~

At the age of 13 my mom gets married to a man named Clive

He asked to adopt me, give me his last name and I thought hey I get money if he died.

Damn I know that sounds harsh and so evil you're thinking that I aint right

But I thought he be just another man stepping in and out of our lives

As time went on I really learned to love him for who he was

He also accepted me, my crazy ways and all my flaws

He never judged me in fact he just shake his head saying look at my child

Now I look back I kind of feel sorry cause damn I was wild

But it was 20 yrs and my Dad never left he was still there

He treated my Mom like a Queen he was a King he was so sincere

But on Christmas day of 2008 he passed away from Cancer

Not my Dad this is isn't true, I don't understand, I need an answer

He was the only man who stepped up and took care of our family

I'm sorry I didn't mean what I said would you please forgive me

My son, my siblings his grandchildren and most of all his wife

How can my Mom survive without him in her life?

I remember how my mom was there at the hospital never left his sight

Although she was scared she still took care of him day and night

I wish this never happened why isn't there a cure

I can remember the pain and suffering he had to endure

The weight loss, the hurt, the chemo the sickness

Nobody deserves this somebody needs to fix this

This is where we begin to question and ask why

Why are the good ones always the ones to quickly die

I wished dealing with death was easier as time goes by

But it seems like it happened just yesterday and you still seem to cry

I wish he had gotten better and he was around

But I do know he is my angel to keep me safe and sound

I just want him to know that he was what you call a man and nothing less

How I'm so sorry that in the beginning I was being so selfish

If you could apologize to someone that you
have not had the chance to, what would you say?

# TIME IS THE MOST THING PEOPLE TAKE FOR GRANTED

I had the opportunity to interview with Daryl "Chill" Mitchell who is a former rapper and now actor. Daryl was in a motorcycle accident and left him paralyzed but it didn't stop him.

The biggest jewel he gave me is that time was the most thing people take for granted. When his accident first happened it took him forever to tie his shoelaces, something that used to take less than a minute. We can take time for many things but we shouldn't take time for granted. Love the ones you love, love yourself and make sure to live and laugh while doing it.

### ~TIME! LIVE, LOVE AND LAUGH!~

Did you hear that so and so died today?
I was just with him around the way
I didn't even give him a hug or told him that I loved him
I was in a rush to get to my job that I was late to anyway
He told me that things were good and that he had plans
Alright No doubt no doubt I'm gonna get up with you my man
Not knowing that was the last time I would hear him speak
Thinking why didn't I embrace him makes me weak
Maybe if I could've stuck around just a little bit more
He would've went a different route and go into that store
That store where he got shot brutally by some punk thief
This can't be real I'm in disbelief
How can live my life without my best friend
We had plans we were going to ride out until the end
The end for him is right now this happened way to fast
Please bring him back I need more memories that can last
We been friends since the age of five
Who do I go to now I need him alive?
He was there for me when my mom's was on drugs
He was my shoulder to lean on he was the definition of love

CONT'D

Was there through my relationships and my heart breaks
Now I'm sitting here crying while my heart aches
My father recently passed too from that demon cancer
I'm looking up to God I'm asking for answers
Two very important people just gone out of my life
How do I wake up in the morning like everything's alright?
In this world while the physical is here
We tend to lose sight of the spirit that is near
That gives us that push that bit of motivation
The inner person, the beauty, the universe, the creation
Time is the most thing that people take for granted
Instead of watering the seeds of knowledge that were planted
Everyone was born with a gift to manifest
The pain, the hurt digs deep in my chest
I'm tired of seeing people settling for less
You deserve to be happy even if you got one minute left
Live love and laugh is what I say quite often
Cause you never know when you be lying in that coffin.

What would you do with your time, if you had 24 hours to live?

```
┌─────────────────────────────┐
│                             │
│    NOW  WHAT  IN            │
│    THE  WORLD  IS           │
│    GOING  ON  IN            │
│    MY  MIND                 │
│                             │
└─────────────────────────────┘
```

# NOW WHAT IN THE WORLD IS GOING ON IN MY MIND

Are you serious? What is going on with my mind? I think I need some help but who do I really turn to? When I ask for help it's only what the world sees fits as assistance. Its not coming from a genuine place so you decide to not seek anything and either you learn how to treat yourself and heal or continue to be toxic. I never went to see a therapist, poetry was my therapy and now I love to hug trees. What is your therapy?

# ~MENTAL HEALTH~

Wake up every day not knowing what's wrong with the effects of my brain
One day I'm feeling good, enjoying my life but then some days I can't maintain.
I manage to go to work every day from 9 to 5
Then there's them days I don't want to open my eyes
It's hard to focus on the reality of my existence
So, I go to the doctor to see if they can give me some assistance
They said David we have to diagnose you with something called bipolar.
We don't know what causes it, but we can give you some meds to help with the
disorder
It can be genetics, a chemical imbalance or even your environment
But be careful of the side effects they can cause depression, anxiety or even
make you violent
But wait doctor I came here to get some help and you're just giving me a
prescription
Told me to take something that will hurt me or maybe cause some infliction
Don't worry, don't worry I have to tell you that just in case
But the more you take them your body will adjust and the problems will erase
Ok so now I am going to start taking this given medication
Because I was never given the proper information
How can they say that there's not a cure for my condition?
I heard there were ways to heal through proper nutrition
So, I'm clueless because I think the correct info is coming from the physician
Not knowing that this is going to cause another addiction
In order to get through my day, I have to have a drink
That's the only thing that gives me the power to think
it helps me become something or someone that I have never been


CONT'D

It helps me to forget the pain that comes within

I don't know what to do I don't know how to deal with the confusion

Oh, but wait once I take the pills the problems will be all an illusion.

Listen everybody is dealing with some hurt and deep-down issues

The problem is we haven't been taught to love ourselves so then our problems seem to continue

There is healing from the illness that is inside of our minds

It's something that we have to find, it's something that takes some time

With the proper knowledge and help from those who have made it through the challenge

You will learn ways for you to deal with things you will learn how to manage

Continue to wake up everyday knowing that you have a purpose

Clear that voice in your head that is causing a disturbance

Connect with people who are also looking to do better

Don't be overwhelmed with society's standards and pressure

Mental illness comes in so many forms but the cycle we must stop repeating

We have become adapted to this behavior but it's up to you to start leading

When your mind starts bugging and you feel like you're out of touch

Take some time to breath and brush the worries into dust

Don't let someone diagnose you with a disease and tell you it can't be treated

You can overcome your issues, you don't have to be defeated.

The hurt, the anger, the depression and anxiety

Even the sickness that comes with the beginning of sobriety

The journey will be rough as you go through this transition

But the journey will be worth it once you start to recondition

Write about your mental health, describe whether its healthy
or not and why. Don't be afraid to let it out.

# HOW DO YOU EVEN COPE?

The thought of someone going through what is most often known as trauma is something people are afraid to talk about. I just like to see it as my journey that way it is easier to talk about and overcome whatever feelings arose from your past. It is something that many are embarrassed and when people see me they often think NAH no way could you have gone through any of those things. How do you manage to smile, how do you even be so free to talk about it? How are you coping today? I choose to be happy and help others in knowing they can always see their light glow no matter how dark some moments have been.

# ~YOU TOUCHED ME~

You touched my body when I told you to stop
You touched my body from the bottom to the top
You touched my body because I wore a short skirt
You touched my body confusing my look with me being a flirt
You touched my body because it looked good to you
You touched my body leaving it black and blue
You touched my body without any of my consent
You touched my body leaving your dreadful scent
You touched my body because you felt as if you were strong
You touched my body and STILL you feel as if you did nothing wrong
You touched my body because it gave your penis a lift
You touched my body because it turned you on when I resist
You touched my body because you thought the younger the better
You touched my body when I cried because it brought you pleasure
You touched my body, you touched my body and yes you touched me
You didn't touch my spirit as it still soars free
You didn't touch my soul from reaching beyond above
You didn't touch my heart because I'm still able to love
You didn't touch my eye from reaching its third point of view
You didn't touch my wings from flying and doing anything I want to do
You didn't touch my hands from giving up the good fight
You didn't touch my power from producing love and light
You didn't touch my tongue that speaks words of healing
You didn't touch my life because yours didn't have any meaning
You touched my body, you touched my body and yes you touched me
But you didn't touch my essence of my supreme divinity

What did you have to cope with in life?
Write down how you managed or how you are trying to deal with it.

# WHO ARE YOU? WHAT DOES YOUR IDENTITY MEAN?

Can you imagine being a young girl, getting molested by multiple men, parents were
on drugs, and let's be honest, the whole community was on drugs (SO THIS IS
NOT TO SHAME MY PARENTS) and you are just
trying to find your way in this thing called life. No one to teach you who you are, or
how to love yourself because it wasn't taught to them.
How in the world do you value yourself as a woman? It took you to go through
not liking yourself and putting yourself through more trouble, to valuing
everything about your worth and knowing who you really are and what you
mean to this thing called life. What is your identity?

# ~WOMAN'S IDENTITY~

Sometimes it's hard for a woman to know her identity

Society makes it easy to become your own worst enemy

Feeling misguided and mislead about your true destiny

Following the crowd instead of doing things differently

They expect us to be reckless and unprofessionally

They want us to be mad and filled with jealousy

Acting devilishly, desperately, and unethically

To make it in the world you must be a celebrity

With a size 2 waist living excessively and expensively

Not to accept yourself the way you're built genetically

How dare you walk with your head high respectfully?

You're not supposed to know what it is to have integrity

They want you to be selfish instead of building collectively

Sometimes it's hard for a woman to know her identity

The power of a woman needs to be used effectively

Knowing your inner beauty and self-worth is a necessity

I know the peer pressure can sometimes weigh heavily

Banned from being who you are you must change cosmetically

As if only physically means more than acting intelligently

Not knowing the true you, who you are authentically

Instead you act more pathetically, offensively with obscenity.

I am not pointing a finger so let me say this apologetically

What if we use our beauty to change the world? Just speaking hypothetically

We are Queens, let your crown shine, present yourself elegantly

We are women, we create life, use that power with intensity

Walk with grace, speak poetically and attract others mentally

There is nothing prettier than woman who can speak intellectually

Woman stand your position in life cause it changes unexpectedly

The world is yours, stay strong and claim your residency

Because sometimes it's hard for a woman to know her identity.

Write about that moment when you found yourself
and what it took to get you to that place.

```
┌─────────────────────────────────┐
│                                 │
│      SO  YOU  DO  ALL           │
│      THIS  TO  FIND             │
│      YOURSELF  AND              │
│      HERE  COMES                │
│      SOCIAL  MEDIA              │
│                                 │
└─────────────────────────────────┘
```

Now look at this thing here called Social Media.

I have to get involved, everyone is on it. I can meet people all over
the world,

I can get in touch with family I have not seen in a while..

But wait, what in the world is going on?

It is a lot deeper than what we expected.

There are so many expectations, there are so many angry people,

why is everyone mad, why is everyone sad?

What is this thing called Social Media?

# ~SOCIAL MEDIA~

Social Media how can I explain it to where it is understanding
You have taken over my life you have been so demanding
Social media you were supposed to help me get through a bad day
Social media I need to know how many notifications did I get today
I need to know do he like it or did he love it
Should I put it on private or should I put it on public
Did he see that picture I posted when I was downtown on vacation
But yo did you see that girl's body I'm trying to fight the temptation
Social media you made this thing it's called private messenger
You tapped my shoulder told me to shoot my shot and and to get at her
So I hit her up she responded I was kind of impressed
But dang here comes that other girl she accepted my request
I'm not going to respond I'm going to wait I got to give her a chance
I want to see if she would be the one to make the first advance
Social media's cool for us to be able to connect with strangers
But you never sat me down and discuss the possible dangers
You never told me they would make jokes because I wasn't to their liking
You didn't tell me that it was cool for us to share videos of us cursing and fighting

CONT'D

Social media I thought you were going to make me feel important
My life connected to the world so I have to paint this portrait
All I wanted to do with you was share some special moments
But how is it that now my friends have become my opponents
It's all your fault because now everything has to be validated
This is no longer fun I am starting to feel agitated
We argue About race and religion
we argue about our skills and position
We take things to the heart and we get offended
I know this is not the way that it was intended
Social media I want to use you in a different way
I want to spread love want to have some positive things to say
I want to show the world that it's okay to show individuality
That we can care about others and show some humanity
Tomorrow when I wake up and I put you on my screen
I'm going to do something different I'm going to change my routine
I'm not going to be concerned with what others have to say
Social media I'm going to help you get through that bad day.

Do you think social media is healthy?
What do you dislike and like about it?

## WE CANT HAVE SOCIAL MEDIA WITHOUT A DOPE SELFIE

How can you not put up a dope selfie?

There is a difference between loving yourself and looking for love from others.

Trust me I get it they have hearts and like reactions and you the goal is to get as many as you can right?

When you decide to put up a selfie, understand it is for you.

It is because of what you have been through and where you are now.

It is because your smile is going to make someone else day. It is because you can

see growth and happiness in your picture. Nothing wrong with a dope selfie but remember to love yourself without having to need acceptance from others.

# ~DOPE SELFIE~

Said you wanna dope selfie said I need to get my fix

Said you want a dope selfie I just need another pic

Said you want a dope selfie, which filter do I pick?

Said you want a dope selfie I'm addicted to this shit


You have to have substance and show that there's something called a brain

If you don't know what I'm saying then here let me explain

We all admire a dope selfie but the addiction becomes in vain

The cameras the needle, the pic is the drug that's injected in your vein

Taking pictures for attention but did I forget to mention that you're more than just a

pose

You're a mother, a friend, a woman of the earth so show us more than the average

knows

Listen I love to throw kisses, and show a dope fit

But there more to our lives than posting a pic

You have to show knowledge, speak with your aura and show them your light

You are responsible for showing others that you're worth more than just a like

How is this even possible when Lisa and Tasha are always showing off their stuff

Their bodies, their handbags and hairstyles, me being different seems like that is not

enough

What is the point of posting a selfie if I can't show off what I got

I want to be the next thing smokin I want others to say I'm Hot

If I don't post the right selfie then I'm gonna be another boring chic

I have all these filters to choose from AND this one gives me nicer lips


CONT'D

Said you wanna dope selfie, Said I need to get my fix
Said you want a dope selfie, I just need another pic
Said you want a dope selfie, which filter do I pick?
Said you want a dope selfie, I'm addicted to this shit

How do we get passed the tons of other pics that we see on a daily
Our boyfriends admire other girls which makes us think that Maybe
Maybe if we looked like that, we can be more in touch with the world
To be liked, to be seen, to be looked at as beautiful not like some regular girl
I can assure you that these selfies will have you imagining things you never knew
Your feelings can be misguided and misled by the images we view
We may even think the couple is super cute because they are always together
Have you saying #goals and thinking their relationship is better
We never see the sadness or hurt that is behind these posted pictures
The low self-esteem or the rotten thoughts behind these hidden figures
So it's up to you to decide who are when you open and close that phone
The real is that your selfie doesn't change the things that go on in your home
So you may want to make believe even if it's for a minute or two
But aren't you eager in knowing who is the real you?
What is your strength, your ability and what is your power?
You are a female, you can run the world if you know how to empower

Said you wanna dope selfie, Said I need to get my fix
Said you want a dope selfie, I just need another pic
Said you want a dope selfie, which filter do I pick?
Said you want a dope selfie, I'm addicted to this shit

What are you thoughts about selfies?
The filters, the likes, the attention.

```
┌─────────────────────────────────┐
│                                 │
│   I   JUST   THINK              │
│                                 │
│   DIFFERENT   AND               │
│                                 │
│   I   LIKE   THAT               │
│                                 │
└─────────────────────────────────┘
```

You can sit there and blame everyone for your life and how it turned out;
however, you are the one responsible for what you do,
how you react and how you relate.
For years I was so mad at the world but not realizing that I was an adult
and I have to take responsibility for the choices I made, the men I dated
and the pain I was inflicting on myself. See the way my mind works....

# ~MY MIND~

The way my mind works is different from many

I like to think positive while others choose to worry

While I'm focused on the solution you still focus on the problem

While I'm raising my vibrations, yours are still at the bottom

While you are still blaming your parents for the life that you made

I took responsibility for my actions and did a spiritual upgrade

I took the fears and lies, and I threw them to the side

I found my passion and my truth which was hiding deep inside

I took a different turn but at first it was for the worst

But I learned to break the cycle from that generational curse

I have a son that I was raising, and I put him through some shit

I was never perfect I am not ashamed to admit

I had to go through the flames to be touched by the heavens

To remove the me from the stress and the deep-down depression

Never for a second do I ever ever question

Why I walked that road and was given certain lessons

Because now I am here to teach and being a poet is my profession

Who would have ever thought that the young girl who wasn't expressive

Can now be here for you to provide a positive message.

How does your mind work?
Are you an overthinker, a pessimist an optimist?

## MEN HAVE HARD TIMES TOO

Who said a woman can not advocate for men?

I want children, men and women to be inspired.

WHY??

I have a 23 year old son that I had to raise and if I can't show him that men
need love too then how would he know?

So this poem I wrote comes from the man's perspective because I know its hard,
especially as a black/brown man,

We as women have so many support groups, and women events that our men get
forgotten about, so this poem is to show you we haven't forgotten about you.

GOT DAMN!!

# ~GOT DAMN~

I'm so stressed. This world just seems to be a Got Damn mess

Rent is $1200 and I make 10 dollars an hour

Disconnection notice I'm about to be without power

No heat in the house cause I live in the slums

Digging in my pockets I keep coming up with crumbs

Baby mommas taking me to court but she gets section 8

If I can't afford to pay I'll be an inmate

With a roommate locked up somewhere upstate

I'm just trying to increase my compensation

Trying to build a foundation; trying to work on my creation

Cause I'm tired of picking cotton on this Got Damn plantation

Not being seen as a human but more of an expectation

Not realizing that this minority man has his limitations

I can take but so much crap from you

I bite my tongue do as you say

and not one time can you pat me on the back and say you did a great job today

Then I come home to nothing but complaints

She wants to debate when all I want is a Got Damn plate

Did you ask me about my day and how I'm doing?

Did you know I got pulled over by the cops because I'm black while moving?

Because apparently I'm a threat is what I was told

The reality is I'm a King that was robbed of his riches and gold

Now I can't even walk down the street with a hoodie on my head to protect me from the cold.

Scared I'm gonna get gunned down cause some folks are just too DAMN bold

Bold enough to take my life, take me away from my kids and my Got Damn wife

I don't have the same opportunities as Bob

They don't consider me or my skin good enough for a promotion at my job

I'm trying to feed my family so sometimes I may have to come up with another hustle

Whether its selling cd's or selling some loosies

I'm a man so I gotta put in that extra muscle

Does it mean that I don't wanna live?? Heck NO

What I am asking is to be left alone

Left alone to survive, to strive, to stay alive

With some Got Damn dignity and some Got Damn pride

Do you think men have it hard too?
What challenges do our men face in society?

## NOT JUST PRIDE
## WE WANT
## JUSTICE TOO

Got Damn we want some justice for all. Tired of fighting,

tired of getting taken advantage of, tired of marching,

tired of being lied to

and used by the system.

Can someone please explain to me WHY are we the target?

Why does it have to be so difficult to succeed

but it's easy for us to fail.

Here is my explanation

# ~JUSTICE FOR ALL~

Mass incarceration, lack of education, false information with no valid explanation

This is our generation we have to show some elevation

so, they can get what they deserve by a little motivation

What if we were taught self-love and meditation?

To help channel and alleviate all the frustration

Of our everyday struggles and our living situations

Don't tell me that this is a figment of my imagination

You're telling me our men can't have a decent place to sleep

A profitable income so he doesn't have to beg to eat

A valuable life that doesn't include lack of quality

Where he can provide for his family not illegitimate but honestly

We want our young kings to walk proudly w/o any confrontation

Where they can wake up and walk through life

with some form of appreciation

We can teach morals, respect and how not to neglect

How to level up and protect, how to manifest and connect

Instead, they are getting locked up for some minor violations

Stuck inside cages because they can't afford the proper representation

But this what we supposed to put our hands to our hearts for this one nation

They say it's under God, indivisible and justice for all... I have a different observation

CONT'D

I see massive incarceration, lack of education, false information with no valid
explanation

So, to our sons that are learning to find their destination

We send you love and light to make it through any situation

In life you have choices there is a way to get out Live for yourself, not in fear, not in
doubt

To our brothers who were recently released after serving some time

Then to be set free because you didn't commit the crime

That has to hit harder than if you were actually guilty Come home, stay focused and plant
that root

for your tree

To our fathers who were unable to provide stability

Because you were never guided on your true capabilities

You were taught how to face your reality and run away from your dreams

Sit back and evaluate on what that really means

Mass incarceration, lack of education, false information with no valid explanation

How can we teach them the many levels to success?

We want jobs not jails to help the minds of the oppressed

How can we teach them love w/o fear of thinking that it's an abnormality?

Thoughts of getting lost to the system or facing some type of inhumane brutality

We were taught to mistreat one another forget unification

We forgot to be role models for the younger generation

They said you're not doing well if you're not affiliated with some big corporation

They said that you have to submit to the system be down with the organization

How can we show love, how can we teach and reach out to our communities?

How can we erase their minds from distrust and provide them with opportunities?

Let's decrease incarceration, provide the proper education,

Stop hiding the information. I hope that I made it clear with my explanation.

Do you have any personal experiences about mass incarceration?
What are your thoughts about the system?

# 2020 PANDEMIC AND NOT BEING ABLE TO BREATHE LITERALLY

Did we walk into 2020 with a clear vision or
did we see what they wanted us to see?
From the pandemic, to being isolated, to watching
another mans life being taken away from us
Now whether it was a plan or not, the fact that they allowed us to see
something to that nature was pretty hard to swallow

## ~I CAN'T BREATHE ~

I can't breathe I can't breathe what did you not understand
Now how can I breathe watching you take the life of another black man
With a knee on his neck as he slowly begs for his life
Got Damn I'm tired of being another lonely black wife
Now I'm afraid for my son as he walks out that door due to the lack of respect
He's not safe in the streets from the ones who supposed to serve and protect
How do I encourage him and tell him he's gonna be fine
When you are constantly targeting us all the damn time
I'm black you are blue and I guess that's what makes you better
I'm sick of yall mess. You expect me to trust you? NEVER
Where are all the good cops the ones who have our backs
The ones who scream out STOP KILLING OFF OUR BLACKS!
Y'all must be somewhere out of this world or somewhere far fetched
How do you sleep at night and how do you think this is ok to accept
I can't breathe I can't breathe is what another man helplessly said
What do you care? When you feel it's just another black man dead
Like the existence of the man made of melanin and gold is not of worth?
The inhumanity of humans makes me sick of this planet earth
You think that there will be this love amongst one another as we breathe the same air
But what is happening and has been happening just doesn't seem to be fair
I'm hurt and I'm upset and those words I don't use
But how much more can we take of being abused

CONT'D

I can't breathe I can't breathe was the words of 2 men that we witnessed on tape

Not knowing how many others senseless acts that our brothers couldn't escape

So do we stay quiet and we mind our own business

Just keep filming these actions and continue to be a witness

Or do we prepare to take back what we so rightfully deserve

Our freedom, our lives, our breathes or is it not our concern

How much more do we scream no justice no peace and continue to protest

Until they take every one of our black man's last breath

Black man you are appreciated and don't get this misunderstood

Black means brown too so let us not start a dispute.

But damn you are worthy, you are loved and most definitely needed

I hate with every cell in my body how you are always mistreated

I wish that you can breathe without others taking that away from you

I breathe life into you and success into everything you do.

I can't breathe I cant breathe is what another man said

I can't believe that again I seen with my own eyes another black man dead.

2020 was a rough year.
How did the murder of George Floyd make you feel?

## THANK YOU FOR THAT DEEP MENTAL PENTETRATION

Do you know what it feels like to be mentally stimulated?
When you can meet someone, you want to grow with on a different level that doesn't consist of material things or selfishness. This can occur in a personal relationship, business or even your fellow community. When I wrote this poem it was directed to a particular person, however finishing this book and going down Memory Lane I have to admit that my friends, my family, my community and I don't like to say fans so I will call you my FAMS, you all have provided me with so much mental penetration, love and support and I dedicate this to you all. I thank you for giving me more than what society expects from people. Thank you for being you and allowing me to be me, many of you seen me throughout this whole journey and stuck with me through every bit of the way and I love you. I hope that this book took you to a place of love, even pain but more importantly the journey of finding peace through it all and allowing yourself to heal.

# ~MENTAL PENETRATION~

Gimme crystals and lessons

Let's discuss our adolescence

As we grow to become blessings

And manifest our progressions

Not focused on possessions

Let's help others out of depression

In a world full of oppression

Let's be each other's protection

Let's be each other's reflection

So to be clear let me just mention

I'm not looking for attention

I'm a woman of comprehension

I don't believe in perfection

But I believe in our connection

Tell me what's your perception

Am I like the rest or am I an exception?

Can we follow in the same direction?

The energy is strong but I'm in need for expression

So you know how I feel and there's never any question

Genuine and loyalty are my only intentions

Level up and connecting into other dimensions

So our vibrations can continue to strengthen

Staying distant from toxic behavior and contagious infections

Together we can be some form of prevention

Learn to master the art of simplicity never complications

So that we can always have the right type of relations

No matter the situation, lets always have communication

Be each other's motivation, put together a formation

So there's never a need for any explanation

I always want you to feel my sincere appreciation,

for providing me with that deep mental penetration.

Write about the time you felt that deep mental penetration.

www.ingramcontent.com/pod-product-compliance
Lightning Source LLC
Chambersburg PA
CBHW060349130626
46553CB00003B/1149